James Pinnock

Benin

The surrounding country, inhabitants, customs, and trade

James Pinnock

Benin
The surrounding country, inhabitants, customs, and trade

ISBN/EAN: 9783337427801

Printed in Europe, USA, Canada, Australia, Japan

Cover: Foto ©Suzi / pixelio.de

More available books at **www.hansebooks.com**

BENIN:

THE SURROUNDING COUNTRY, INHABITANTS, CUSTOMS, AND TRADE.

A Lecture delivered before the Geographical Societies of Liverpool,
Newcastle-on-Tyne, &c.,

By

MR. JAMES PINNOCK.

—

LIVERPOOL:

THE "JOURNAL OF COMMERCE" PRINTING WORKS 9, VICTORIA STREET.

—

1897.

ALFRED L. JONES, Esq., J.P.

Photo. by C. E. Medrington.

I DEDICATE this reprint of a Lecture delivered before the Geographical Societies of Liverpool and Newcastle-on-Tyne, &c., on " Benin, the Surrounding Country, Inhabitants, Customs, and Trade," to my friend,

ALFRED L. JONES, Eso., J.P.,

who has spent his life in developing steam communication and trade with West Africa.

I here take the opportunity of acknowledging my indebtedness to the proprietors of *The Graphic* and *Black and White* for the illustrations of scenes in Africa which they have kindly supplied to me.

JAMES PINNOCK.

LIVERPOOL,
February, 1897.

BENIN:

The Surrounding Country, Inhabitants, Customs, and Trade.

A LECTURE DELIVERED BEFORE THE
GEOGRAPHICAL SOCIETIES OF LIVERPOOL, NEWCASTLE-ON-TYNE, &C.,

BY

Mr. JAMES PINNOCK.

It is said that Great Britain is never without her little war. As far as Africa is concerned this appears to be the case, and undoubtedly will be for some time to come, as she cannot expect to rule and be always at peace with the inhabitants of her ever-increasing dominions in that quarter of the globe any more than a man with fifty or one hundred thousand pounds annual income derived from landed estate can be at peace with all his numerous tenants or free from disputes or lawsuits.

Only one hundred miles distant from Benin is the most flourishing and ever-developing British colony on the whole Western Coast of Africa, viz., Lagos, and this country was only taken into our family of colonies on the 6th of August, 1861. The trade of Lagos has increased almost beyond belief, particularly during the last year or two, in the very valuable product of rubber, which is worth nearly £200 per ton.

When my friend, the late Mr. McCoskry, went to Lagos as recently as 1851, the European residents then numbered only 20 Portuguese and four Englishmen; now there are about 200

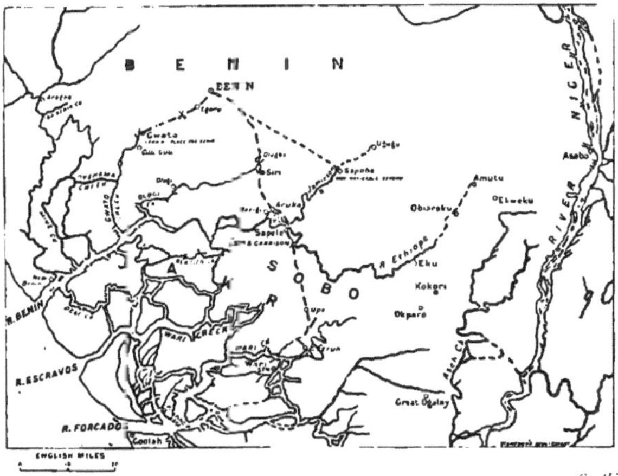

B E N I N

BENIN

Aragba

Gwato
Gill Gili

Oba

IBINI
Idugbo

Sari

BEN-B Aruku
Sapele
Sum & Casa lbor

Obiarebug

Okudbo

Sapohe

Amutu

Asabo

Ekweku

R. Ethiope

Eku

J A K R I

S O B O

Kokgri

Okparo

R. BENIN

WARI CREEK

R. ESCRAVOS

R. FORCADO

Coolah

Great Ogolay

R I V E R   N I G E R

ENGLISH MILES

CHART OF THE NIGER COAST PROTECTORATE, DECEMBER, 1896.

Graphic.

resident Europeans. The gross value of the export in 1858 was £191,892 10s. (under £200,000), palm oil being then valued at £40 per ton. Last year the export would approximately reach £1,250,000, with palm oil valued now at one-half, or about £20 per ton.

I omitted to mention that the day succeeding the cession of Lagos to the British Crown by King Docemo, a French naval officer entered the roadstead of Lagos, and, hearing of the cession, departed very vexed. What a happy circumstance we were a day in advance, and had France not annexed it Germany would undoubtedly have done so, as their merchants had a strong footing there and have still, some millions of gallons of cheap fiery spirits being annually imported into that colony.

I hope I am not making a divergence from our subject, which is Benin, but to which I must remind you is coupled "the surrounding country," and I want to point out to you, ladies and gentlemen, that as such prosperity has come to Lagos under the British rule, we may, I feel assured, expect equally good results by attaching the whole of the Benin country to our African possessions. We are happily situated in this respect, as no question whatever can possibly arise with either France, Germany, or any other country, for not a single traveller of these or any other nationality has ever put foot in that country, which can hardly be said of any other spot on earth—I mean a country of any great extent. There is no question of any genuine or bogus treaty or concession to any one with any king, chief, or native, excepting one only which I hold myself for seventy square miles for mining rights, &c., &c.

The country is a rich one, and in every respect, I think, better and more fertile than Lagos, but of course wants developing and the advantages of some years of civilization and British rule.

I have pointed out to you Lagos has taken from the year 1861 (when it was attached as a colony) to attain its present proud position 35 years, and Benin will of course also take time to develop in a similar manner.

CHIEF NANA'S CANOE, BENIN RIVER.

SAFELI

TIMBERRY

THE NARROWS.

Graphic.

When I first went to Lagos, some years prior to the first visit of the late great explorer, Sir Richard Burton, it was the temporary home of Portuguese and Brazilian slave supercargoes, as well as a few traders; and human skulls were to be seen placed on tall bamboo sticks stuck in the mud on the banks of the river.

In the general European scramble for a slice of "the black man's garden" (as we now call Africa) surely our Premier or his Cabinet will not allow this rich, unapportioned country to remain so any longer; it is England's *future* wealth and greatness our legislators have to study, as well as the *present*. Had this been more thought of and acted upon a quarter to half a century ago the English flag might now have been floating over nearly the whole of the African Continent— certainly over three - fourths of it. Within the last half century the whole of the Western portion and for a thousand miles inland had no more thought or care from our Government than a pauper's grave. I need not tell you that the African Continent bids fair in the future to equal any other country on earth. You have seen yourselves what the result so far of the opening out of South Africa has been, and upon the authority of one of the leading mine-owners there given to me direct (I refer to my friend, the late Mr. Mylchreest, called the "Diamond King," who died only a few weeks since) " we have yet," he said, " barely scratched the earth."

I am inclined to go, perhaps you will think, to too great lengths when I tell you I believe Africa will be in the future all that India or America is to-day. They say history repeats itself. What was it in Cleopatra's time, or when the foundation stones of the Pyramids were laid, or anterior thereto? He would have been a bold prophet who could have predicted one hundred years ago the America of to-day or the Cape when I visited it in 1855.

But my text is Benin, and does not comprise the whole of the African Continent, so I must ask you to pardon me if I have gone too far afield. It is my enthusiasm for that great country of the future that carries me along.

Graphic

A Street in Benin City.

Dahomey lies but a short distance from Benin ; there is only a difference of 1° latitude and of 2° 20″ longitude, and see what the French have recently done there. The King of Dahomey, whose capital is or was Abomey, at times, on the occasion of great state ceremonies, slaughtered wholesale very many more of his countrymen than the King of Benin. I have heard of as many as 1,200 being killed at one great festival in honour of the deceased king, and all sent to serve their master in the next world and a message given to each one to deliver to him. The French have swept the murderous king and all his savage court away, and peace and order now reign over that country. Porto Nova, which is the shipping port of Dahomey, has now its custom house and officials, and business is conducted upon European lines. Early in the 'fifties a Brazilian slave super-cargo residing there had more than once a present sent him of 500 slaves by the King of Dahomey.

Africa will be in the future, as it is to-day (though to a very much greater extent than at present), a grand outlet and home for our surplus population—I refer here, of course, to the healthier parts of Africa and to the highlands, and not the mangrove belt of the Oil Rivers. Britons when they go abroad go to stay and make their mark, as they have done in America and are still doing in Australia, New Zealand, the Cape, and other great dependencies of the British Empire. Britons are like hardy plants, transferred to another soil they take root and acclimatise themselves wherever they go. Not like the Frenchman, though I would be very sorry to say one word that would hurt the feelings of anyone belonging to that great nation ; but Frenchmen, I think it is almost universally acknowledged, are not good colonists, as they have an over-weening love of home and country, and do not care for too long a banishment from same, together with their boulevards and cafés, &c., but in establishing new colonies or extending others France proceeds on the sound principle. By sending her best men, naval and military, she shows her force and impresses the natives before treating ; her warlike imperial policy contrasts strongly with our puritanical peaceful missions which have

Black and White. TYPICAL STREET SCENE, OLD BENIN CITY.

Black and White. MANGROVE CREEK, BENIN RIVER.

brought about the recent lamentable massacre at Benin, and
which has resulted in the sacrifice of upwards of 200 human
lives.

To the late Macgregor Laird is due the great honour of
opening up not only the Niger River but the whole of the
West Coast of Africa to trade and commerce with this country,
and to bring about steam communication with that part of the
world. By his almost individual efforts he founded and
started the African Steamship Company in 1852, my intimate
acquaintance with which commenced six years later, or 1858,
though I had the pleasure of knowing him years before. The
fleet then consisted of only three small steamers of 600 tons
each, the "Armenian," "Athenian," and "Ethiope," the only
steamers of any nationality then running to the West Coast of
Africa. This then represented the whole of the steam tonnage
engaged in that trade, and with a very large subsidy from
Government for carrying the mails, viz., £2,500 per sailing
with a contract speed then of only eight knots per hour; and
simply with a view of showing you the enormous growth of the
trade of that part of the world, the African Steamship
Company have now no less a tonnage than 124,263 tons, whilst
the competing or sister company have a further tonnage of
43,040 tons, all this last-named confined solely to the one trade.
The mercantile world and public generally give most of the
credit to Mr. A. L. Jones, the head of the firm who manages
both these huge concerns, for this great subsequent development. He has been connected with it—I was going to say
since his infancy—well, since his boyhood, and still is every
hour of the day, and it is to his foresight, enterprise, and
energy the trade has reached its present colossal proportions.
Only the other day there left this port the largest ship ever
built on the Tyne, the "Milwaukee," built by Messrs. Swan
and Hunter for Mr. Jones. The same firm have also completed
very recently steamers for service at Lagos in connection with
the same shipping company, and other ships are also building
here and at Middlesbro' for the same firm. I was at the launch
of one of the handsomest steamers ever sent to the West

Graphic.

Graphic.

African Coast only the other day, also built for the same gentleman ; I refer to one built at Middlesbro' by that eminent firm, Sir Raylton Dixon's Company.

Our trade with the West African Coast can clearly be traced back 400 years, if not longer, and it is only now daily making vast strides towards development, and our countrymen are gradually pushing their way into the more salubrious interior, where they are opening up new and unexploited sources of wealth. When the white population settle at a good altitude above the sea level, with greater facilities of locomotion and intercourse inland, they will retain their health and energy, *at least* very much better than at present, or on a footing with residents in India.

Those rivers of Africa known as the Oil Rivers, situated in the Bight of Benin and Biafra, and extending from Lagos to Fernando Po, are simply the sewers of Africa—the washings and waste of the interior, a labyrinth of creeks with a great depth of black, fœtid mud, made up principally of decayed vegetable matter subject more or less to the ebb and flow of the tide, the water consequently very brackish to salt, where nothing will grow but the mangrove, with its innumerable suckers. What would be the result if the people of England lived on such a site and with such death-dealing surroundings ?

This state of things exists over a belt extending about sixty miles (varying here and there) inland from the Atlantic Ocean, and those who have traded backwards and forwards there for the whole of their lives have lived and died in the belief that this was a fair sample of that part of Africa. For many years this was my confirmed opinion, until I built at Birkenhead a steamer for myself and set about exploring the interior, and endeavoured to ascertain what stood behind this almost impenetrable fringe of mangrove and mud. I was more than rewarded, as, after leaving Benin and proceeding for days through innumerable winding and tortuous creeks, I at last reached the Niger by this route ; the way is made comparatively easy to-day since it has now become known. I was fired at from some villages where the waterway was only about

THE LATE MR. KENNETH CAMPBELL, VICE-CONSUL, AND KROOMEN.
(Massacred in the march to Benin)

Black and White.

THE LATE DR. R. H. ELLIOTT, AND SERVANTS.
(Massacred with late Benin expedition).

Black and White.

twice the width of any ordinary canal, the inhabitants imagining I had either come to take their country or was on a slave-raiding expedition, the natives of some villages running after the steamer as far as practicable, throwing lumps of clay and anything they could lay their hands on. This puzzled me considerably, but I ascertained subsequently it was the long trail of black smoke issuing from the funnel of my steamer lying in the atmosphere over their villages they were frightened at, and they fancied it would bring disaster upon them in the shape of smallpox, a disease which carries off great numbers, and they were exorcising or driving the evil spirit of the thing away. At other places where the natives were not so frightened I saw them on the banks hastily picking up the most horrible specimens of fat mangy puppies and paddling quickly, trying to catch the steamer to barter the same for beads, tobacco, or rum, believing they (the dogs) were a toothsome morsel for the white man's palate.

Steaming later on I came to the broad waters of the Niger, which at this point was fully a mile wide, and, proceeding day by day towards the interior, frequently grounding, and with a powerful current to contend against, anchoring of course every night at sunset, I reached a beautiful varied country with lofty mountains here and there of every variety of formation, with occasional high cliffs. I thought what a glorious country Africa was after all, and I cannot tell you how all my previously-conceived ideas of Africa were revolutionised. But now I find I am getting too far away from Benin. Possibly some day I may make the great Niger River an entirely separate subject, as I must do, for there is another altogether separate war at the present moment being carried on in that country under the English flag or under an English chartered company.

In this recent terrible disaster at Benin we lost not only five European Government officers, which included the Acting Consul-General Phillips, Captain Maling, Vice-Consuls Crawford and Campbell, and Dr. Elliott, also two European traders, Messrs. Powis and Gordon, and in addition thereto 200 friendly natives and Kroomen, all of whom were most murderously

LIEUT.-COLONEL BRUCE HAMILTON
(Commanding the Punitive Expedition).

Graphic.   *Photo by Fripp, Cape Town.*

CAPTAIN A. M. BOISRAGON
(Commandant of the Protectorate's Force. One of the survivors of the Benin massacre).

Black and White.

THE LATE CAPTAIN A. J. MALING
(Of the Protectorate's Wing. One of the victims of the Benin disaster).

Black and White.   *Photo. by J. Thomson.*

THE LATE MR. POWIS
(Taken prisoner and massacred by the King of Benin).

Black and White.   *Photo. by Arthur Weston.*

butchered, not to mention Captain Boisragon and Vice-Consul Locke, whom you have read fortunately escaped wounded after terrible sufferings endured during five days wandering in the bush, adjacent to the country of these pitiless, bloodthirsty savages of Benin City.

Naturally all our sympathy has gone forth for the loss of this noble band of European victims, who were bound solely on a mission of peace to the sable potentate of these unsavoury realms; but our great sympathy should also be extended—almost, if not quite, as much to the large body of followers who were slaughtered with them, and which, as far as we learn at present, consisted largely of that race of men known as Kroomen—far away the finest in every respect of the whole of the tribes of Western Africa. We took them there ; they followed our heroic countrymen faithfully and fearlessly and unarmed, and got sacrificed in the awful trap into which our officials led them. Knowing these men so well as I do after a long experience, my heart goes out to their sad memory and to their numerous friends and relatives left to mourn their loss. We must remember they have fathers, mothers, brothers, sisters, and children like ourselves. Nowhere have I found any notice of sympathy being expressed for them in any English print. It would be a most gracious act, and do an infinite amount of good and have a lasting impression in that country, if some acknowledgment was made by our Government.

Brass River was so called because the favourite article of trade there in early times was brass pans—large, open, circular dishes, sometimes known in the trade as " Neptunes."

Again : Fernando Po takes its name from the old Portuguese explorer, Fernão de Poo.

The Ramos River, from the northern entrance of which extends a spit named " Murder Spit," from the fact that it was here that two most promising young officers and a boat's crew belonging to H. M.S. " Avon " were most barbarously murdered by the natives whilst engaged surveying, &c., &c. This was in April, 1846. Their names were Henry Pennington and O. A.

Black and White

THE LATE MR. T. GORDON
(Massacred with the late Benin expedition)

Black and White.

Capt. Boisragon.   Mr. R. F. Locke, Vice-Consul.

THE SURVIVORS OF THE BENIN DISASTER.

Winstanley. The Pennington River and Winstanley outfalls
were named after these officers.

The Middleton River was so christened after the assistant
surgeon of the "Avon."

The Nun, or Akassa River. Here stood the old Portuguese town of Akassa, long since entirely swept away. A tomb
was reported to have been found there, bearing the date 1635.

Escardos River, the first river south of Benin, was really
named the Escravos or Slave River, the modern name, Escardos,
being a corruption thereof.

Bonny takes its name from the native word Obani, and so
I could continue the derivation of the most of the rivers of this
part of Africa, but I will trouble you no longer hereon.

That intrepid traveller, Belzoni, who unfortunately left his
bones at Benin in 1823, was then known as "Belzoni of the
Pyramids" for his researches in Egypt.

Benin was visited as far back as 1485 by Alfonso de Aviro,
a Portuguese traveller, and it was again visited in 1553 by
Captain Thomas Wyndham, so you see it almost assumes the
dignity of what some might term classic ground.

When travelling some distance inland from the Benin
River *a different route to Benin City*, I came across a race of
people, or a number of them, with long tails. I see several
eyes fixed upon me in incredulous astonishment, but, nevertheless,
I must still unblushingly adhere to my statement. You might
tell me to produce one and take him round the country for
exhibition. I am afraid I should be denounced as an impostor,
as the tails of these savages are *not* provided by nature.
Nevertheless, these people suffer under an imaginary wrong : not
being born with what seems to them such necessary appendage.
They themselves make good the deficiency by affixing to the
lower part of their back a natural cow's tail as it is severed
from the animal's body, dried, &c., with all the hair, &c.,
remaining, secured to their bodies by native fibrous rope.

I first came across a number engaged in tilling the land in
a stooping position without a vestige of clothing, and the sight
impressed me as weird, and by no means becoming. On

THE LATE ACTING-CONSUL GENERAL, PHILLIPS

(Massacred *en route* to Benin City).

Black and White.

Photo by A. Hollis, Barrow-in-Furness.

THE LATE MAJOR P. W. G. COPLAND-CRAWFORD

(Massacred *en route* to Benin City).

Black and White.

Photo by Barsana.

making inquiries why they so adorned themselves, *if adorn-ment it can be called*, they told me that as it was useful to cows and other animals for brushing the flies and insects from their bodies it was of equal advantage to them. They at once demonstrated it by beating off the flies at that moment settling on one man's face, and the other being bitten by a large brown mangrove fly in the small of the back *he went for the same* most effectually at once, and, picking the blood-sucking insect from the ground, considered *that* the crowning argument in favour of the fashion of his country.

Few, if any, white men have traversed this particular line of country, as I fail to find it anywhere recorded; but my present resident agent at Benin (Mr. Swainson) and one or two others have been amongst them. As reference to these people has not appeared in print, it appears never to have been brought under the notice of the world.

It indeed seems strange, but in this very thriving British colony of Lagos—the "Liverpool of West Africa," as so many of its colonists are fond of calling it, and which is, as I have before mentioned, only one hundred miles from Benin— we had the same trouble when we rescued it from a similar barbaric state. It is almost forgotten now, but on the 25th November, 1850, a force of 260 men from Her Majesty's ships, in 23 boats, crossed the bar under the command of the late Commander Forbes, of H.M.S. "Philomel." This force landed, but, though preceded by a flag of truce carried by the late Consul Beecroft, were met by about 5,000 armed natives, who kept up a sharp fire from behind the houses and trees, which compelled our men to retreat with the loss of two killed and several wounded.

To redeem this disaster and to punish the truculent natives a second expedition one month later crossed Lagos Bar. It consisted of 400 bluejackets and marines from four of Her Majesty's ships lying outside in the roadstead, and was led by Commodore R. W. Bruce, of H.M.S. "Penelope." The natives, hidden by the tall grasses and walls of vegetation, fired unseen upon our band of assailants, who eventually came off victorious,

Graphic.   THE VICE-CONSULATE AT WARRI, ON THE BENIN RIVER.

Black and White.   CONSULATE, ROYAL NIGER COAST PROTECTORATE.

but we lost 16 men killed and 71 wounded, being nearly 25 per cent. of our force of 400. The destruction of the natives was, I need not say, much greater.

I leave to your imaginations the transformation scene made in Lagos in 45 years. I dare not detain you now by dwelling on it ; I only wish you to bear in mind what we may not expect in Benin in a similar length of time, having a river accessible to all steamers which Lagos has not, and united, as I trust Lagos and Benin may be in the future, by railway, telegraph, and telephone. Benin is at present without any of these, or even cable communication.

Benin has been well known to European nations for very many years, when it was one of the leading ports on the West African Coast for the export of slaves. The ancient name for the River Benin was Rio Formosa, the Portuguese for "beautiful river." Why it should have been so called is beyond comprehension, unless it was for the great number of slaves of a superior marketable character to be obtained there. The trade carried on by Europeans was, I am sorry to say, almost entirely confined to the horrible traffic in human flesh, or such as we now consider it. It appears almost incredible, but I find even at the date mentioned, 1st September, 1702, in Benin River the Portuguese had not only a lodge but a church about a mile or more from the river mouth, called Agberi.

Mr. Bosman writes : " The ships all sailed about sixty miles inland from the ocean, and which I conclude was either Gwato or Sapeli." He described the sickness and mortality of the Europeans on board the ships then as very great.

I would not wish to alarm any who have friends in that part of the world, or friends of those who are going there, as the state of things is very much altered now. The accommodation for the health and comfort of all has been revolutionised, to say nothing of the present superiority of food, &c. As a re-assurance to those who may have friends and relatives who will take part in the coming expedition, I may mention that during all my travels and explorations in that part of the world— and it embraced the whole region from the River Gambia to

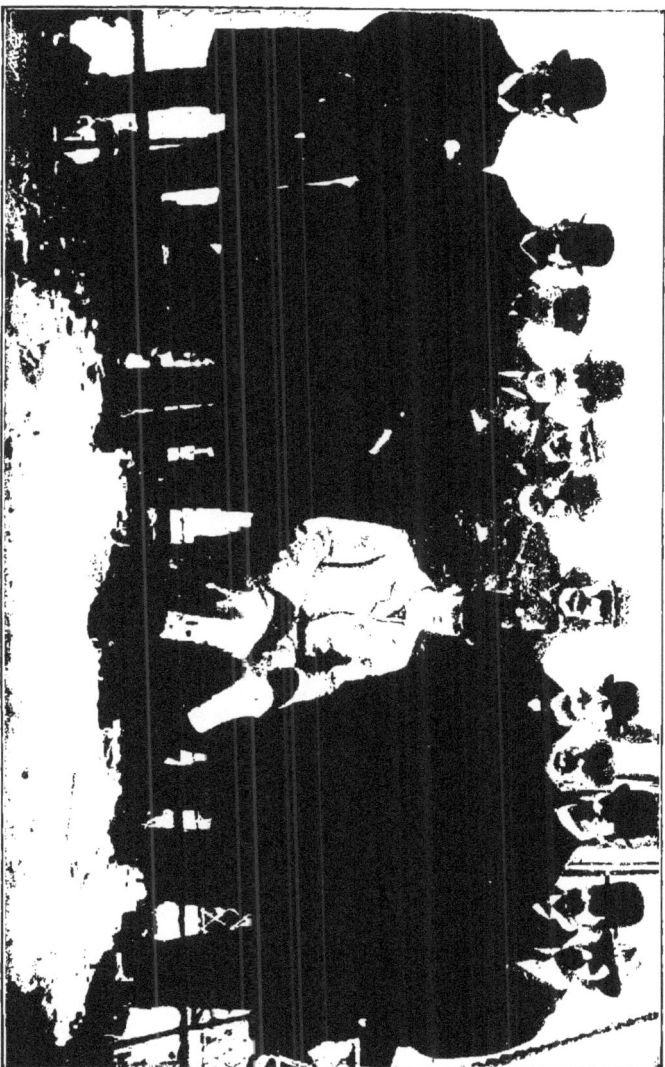

PROTECTORATE OFFICIALS LEAVING LIVERPOOL PER R.M.S. "BATHURST," SATURDAY, 16TH JANUARY, 1897.

Mr. Whitehouse.   Capt. Norman   Capt. Walker
        Dr. Roth.   (—Sadiar—)   Mr. Copland-Crawford.   Dr. Altman.   Consul-General R. D. Moor.   Lieut.-Col. Hamilton.   Mr. O'Farrell.
            Mr. Ledsley.

Photo by Robinson & Thompson, Liverpool.

Fernando Po, and far away into the interior, even as far distant
as the city of Beda, where I had gone to pay a visit to the Emir
of Nupe (kingdom of Sockatoo), also to Egga, which has
recently been destroyed by the Niger Company's forces, at both
of which places I resided for some time—I never remember to
have suffered from one single day's sickness, but then I was
always known and written of as " the man with the iron consti-
tution." I lived in Sierra Leone ten years, and only had ten
days' sickness during my long residence there.

It is against the Emir of Nupe and the city of Beda that
the present expedition of the Royal Niger Company is directed,
and later on they will attack Ilorin. Benin and the country for
a great distance around it is under the jurisdiction of the Niger
Coast Protectorate, and I would wish to particularly mention
and point out here that the Royal Niger Company is a totally
different enterprise altogether to the Niger Coast Protectorate.
The Protectorate is a direct arm of the British Government,
and solely controlled by our Government, whilst the Royal
Niger is a chartered company solely governed and directed
by a very limited body of directors in London.

Mr. Bosman, the then agent for the Dutch Slave Company
at Benin, tells us that at a village close to Gwato, near the
scene of the recent massacre, some years previous to 1702 there
stood an English factory and a Dutch factory belonging, as he
puts it, to " our Company," meaning the large Dutch company,
but that they amalgamated and worked later on with the
respective factors, agents, and clerks as one concern. There
was then, in addition to the trade in slaves, some trade in ivory,
the elephants being then far more numerous and coming nearer
the coast.

Nowhere does Mr. Bosman make any mention whatever of
any human sacrifices at that period at Benin, and he has
written at very great length from that place. Hence the conclusion that I draw is that it did not then exist, and the slaves
could be dealt with by their masters to so much better
advantage by bartering them for European goods which the
ships brought them, and which ships comprised Dutch, Spanish,

Black and White.

Sacrificial Chamber, or "Ju-Ju House," Benin City.

Portuguese, and English nationalities. The custom then in dealing for slaves was much the same as it is to-day in dealing with the same people for produce. The slave trade, I may mention, exists over the greater portion of Africa much the same to-day as it did any time during the last thousand years, Benin and the surrounding country included.

The first steam vessel to enter the Benin River was the "Ethiope," of 30 horse-power—built in 1839 by Mr. Robert Jamieson, merchant, of Liverpool — after the failure of Mr. Macgregor Laird's Niger expedition, which sailed from Liverpool on 19th July, 1832, composed of the two steamers "Quorra," of 40, and the "Alburkah," of 16 horse-power, with Mr. Laird, Mr. Oldfield, Mr. Lander, and others, some of whom I knew well. Mr. Robert Jamieson took a very great interest and invested a large sum of money in a most praiseworthy endeavour to explore the Rio Formosa or River Benin, and to try if other and better channels could not be found to the Niger. This vessel (the "Ethiope"), it will be interesting for you to know, was commanded by one Mr. Beecroft, to whom this country is indebted for many most valuable explorations in this region. There are two rivers, tributaries to the Benin, known as the Jamieson and the Ethiope, named after the steamer in question and her owner. The "Ethiope" entered the Benin River in April, 1840. Captain Beecroft pioneered and pushed his way up both these streams as far as possible ; one he ascended 50 and the other 70 miles, and he describes them as winding, bold, and beautiful, and a depth of water varying from three to six fathoms. Ultimately he had to return in consequence of floating meshes of aquatic vegetation, not from any deficiency of depth of water, but which he could not penetrate except by a tedious and laborious process of cutting his way through.

By way of a slight digression I must inform you that two years prior to the advent and explorations of the steamer "Ethiope" two of the officers of a vessel named the "Warree," also belonging to Mr. Jamieson, of Liverpool, took their boat and were paddled by Kroomen up the Gwato Creek to Gwato, and thence were carried in hammocks in a north-easterly

THE LATE MACGREGOR LAIRD, ESQ.

(The principal Pioneer in opening up the Niger, and the Founder of the African Company).

direction through a finely-wooded and in some places very beautiful country (at least so they described it at the time) to the city of Benin. These two men, Messrs. Moffat and Smith, found the city then in the same horrible state of savagery and butchery as it is to-day.

When the transport of slaves from Africa to the West Indies and elsewhere became unlawful, trade in the products of the country had to be resorted to to take the place of the slave trade, and has now developed into one of vast proportions, and which, if it had had formerly more fostering care and attention from our authorities at home, would already be much greater. I remember being the first to ship home, from this or neighbouring river of Warri, palm kernels ; the first year it was only 6 tons, the next 60 tons, and the year following 600 tons, and now it amounts to several thousand tons per annum, divided between the different houses trading there. The King of Old Benin allows no palm kernels to be sent from his dominions or to pass through ; the same applies to rubber, gum, &c. All these valuable products are allowed to rot, as no use whatever is made of them.

In 1870 I built a steamer of about 200 tons carrying capacity, which was called after Benin River, viz., the " Rio Formosa." I personally navigated her about these various rivers and creeks, and surveyed and opened out for the first time in history an adjacent river called the " Forcardos," the largest and finest estuary on the whole of the West African Coast. Though there is a safe and good channel over the bar for any of the mail steamers or Her Majesty's first-class cruisers, and a saving of nearly one hundred miles in getting to the European factories and consulate station at Warri, in place of, as previously, getting there by a long and tedious route viâ Benin, it was a long time before I could get any one to attempt it, and Benin was, and is, inaccessible to anything but a very small light draught branch steamer. Ultimately I succeeded in persuading the master of one of Messrs. Elder, Dempster and Co.'s small branch river steamers to allow me to pilot him into and over it. I need not say I did so successfully ; but it

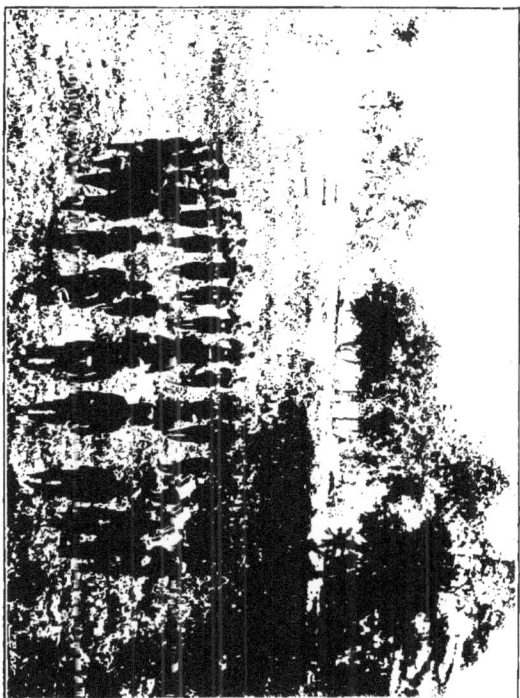

Black and White.

ROYAL NIGER COAST PROTECTORATE FORCE BAND.

was not until a long time afterwards one of the regular
steamers would venture to try it. Now it swarms with vessels
of every size, and has become a depôt for all the steamers going
to and from the West Coast, and any steamer can go through a
creek communicating with Benin, whereas previously the only
entrance to Benin was over the bar of that river for vessels of
the lightest possible draught.

Neither in Warri nor New Benin, as the latter is
termed at the present moment to distinguish it from the
charnel house City of Benin, is there, or has there been in
all my experience, which extends over forty years, any
cannibalism, and only on very rare and exceptional occasions
any human sacrifices. Neither New nor Old Benin,
Warri, Sapeli, or Forcardos have ever had any English
or foreign missionaries, Scripture readers, or schoolmasters,
black or white—nothing since the Portuguese in 1700 to 1720.
Whether the natives are better or worse for this I must leave to
others, personally I would say much the worse for their absence ;
but there are some nice, upright, honourable black men and
women amongst them that I have a great respect for. One man
whose name I would like to mention is Chief Dore, and who I
am sure will lend this coming expedition most valuable
assistance ; also Du-du and two of the sons of my old friend
Nyowrie, chief of Warri, named Oagbey and Ocoro; but these
are details I must not bother you with.

The most powerful chief ever known in Benin was Alluma,
the late father of the deposed Chief Nana. He had about
3,000 slaves and innumerable wives. I once went on a visit to
him and to dine with him. Nana was not allowed then to be
seated at his father's table or in his presence, but waited upon
us. Going outside I saw a large number of men all hand-
cuffed and chained to a stout projecting handrail running
round the building, standing about three feet from the ground,
all with their ears cut off, not with a pair of scissors, but taken off
clear from the head with a razor. It was truly a horrible sight ;
the lacerated parts festering and covered with flies of every
sort and size, and the poor fellows not able to raise a hand to

THE LATELY-DEPOSED CHIEF NANA,
OF BENIN

(Now prisoner in exile on the Gold Coast).

Black and White.

CHIEFS FRAGONIE DU-DU, AND DORE, AT BENIN

(All loyal and friendly good men).

Black and White.

brush them away, kept in a standing position, unable to sit or
lie down, and exposed outside to the broiling sun by day and
the millions of mosquitoes and sand-flies by night. I asked
Alluma the cause of this atrocity, and he told me these men
had been sent by him to the distant British colony of Lagos
(a thing that did not occur twice in a lifetime), and on their
return they had been describing to their fellow-slaves the
wonders they had seen, and that in Lagos all men were free,
there were no slaves there, a thing almost too wonderful for
anyone of them to grasp, as they had never heard of any such
spot on earth. They were also describing, as they termed it,
the white man's great ju-ju house, meaning thereby the church
at Lagos. These men did not preach one word of mutiny or
escape ; when in Lagos themselves they could have instantly
claimed their freedom and never returned ; but they came
back to their old servitude, and simply for the recounting of
their experiences they were so fearfully mutilated.

The trade has always been carried on by barter, and we
give them in exchange for their products, gin, rum, tobacco,
guns, powder, matchetts, and some cotton goods and silk hand-
kerchiefs, &c.

Our bluejackets and the forces of the Protectorate will, we
are quite sure, clear this Gehenna which is at present a disgrace
to the whole world (civilised and uncivilised), and our forces
when they occupy Benin will have to burn continual fires to
clear the atmosphere from the pestilental effluvia arising from
the dead bodies of the continual daily sacrifices of human
beings.

I would like to add that we are much indebted to Mr.
Ralph Moor, the Consul-General of the Niger Coast Protectorate, and his able staff for the very excellent manner in which
the exceedingly arduous duties devolving upon them have been
performed, and in such a very trying climate.

With respect to the religion of the inhabitants of these
regions (if religion it can be called), a rather wide distinction
must be drawn between that of the now infamous, horrible city
of Old or Black Benin and the inhabitants of New Benin and

THE JU-JU AND ITS IDOLATORS.

WORSHIP OF THE JU-JU.

the Benin and Warri Rivers, and those residing in the neighbourhood of the European trading stations or within touch of the same.

The former is a system of fetishism, the fetish priests exercising an unlimited power over both the King and his subjects. Their rites consist of innumerable sacrifices of fowls, goats, bullocks, and very many innocent human beings of almost every age and of both sexes. These sacrifices are made for any and every reason—sometimes to commemorate the death of the late King, again as an offering to him at frequent odd times, also to stop too much rain, and again to bring rain when the country has too long suffered from drought. The King, under the advice of his fetish priests, having decided on the closing of a certain adjacent market or the road leading to the same, sacrifices a man and divides him nearly in half, stretching his body across the path to denote the road is closed, and that anyone disobeying will come to evil or meet a similar fate.

A friend (the late Captain White) going from Gwato to Benin, on a visit to the King, found by the roadside some men standing in an upright position against some trees, strangled by a rope drawn round their necks to the trees. On his enquiring of the King why these awful atrocities were committed, he was told it was in honour of his visit, and to propitiate the goodwill of the gods on their interview. Many of both sexes are sacrificed to keep up the retinue of servants or slaves in attendance upon their late royal master *across the border.* Beyond the few facts I have recorded, no one has ever attempted to unravel the mysteries of the fetish worship.

Men and women who are crucified are fastened, some of them high up in the trees, secured only by the wrists and ancles, and, from information I gathered from the people, they take various lengths of time to die. I have heard of even as long, occasionally, as ten to fourteen days, but I cannot tell how true it is. Possibly some of the victims have been inured to great hardships from their infancy, and at times been

A WOMAN CRUCIFIED AT BENIN

Graphic.   (A Sacrifice to the God of Rain).

Black and White.   GRAND BASSA JU-JU MAN.

subjected to long intervals of hunger and thirst, which might account for their lasting a long time.

The bodies so hung at a considerable height wither and dry up and mummify, and do not decay as in the ordinary course of nature, or as they would in almost twenty-four hours in that climate if lying on the ground. I must leave to the scientific to explain this. It has occurred to me whether it is above the range of the egg-depositing fly or insect, or the combined drying influence of the sun and wind.

The religion or doctrines of the inhabitants of the region bordering on the coast consists of the belief in a future state. To describe it is difficult, as it appears so vague and undefined. One of their principal gods is Malaku, the God of Water. In traversing the creeks it is a very usual sight to see pieces of white baft, a young live chicken tied by the leg to a branch, &c., &c., placed there as an offering to this deity so that he may appease the turbulence of the water and permit their canoes to pass in safety. One often sees several large canoes in company proceeding down the river nearly to the seaboard, with flags flying, tom-toms beating, men dancing, and forty slaves paddling (twenty on either side); this is usually some leading chief going to worship Malaku, which consists of dancing, singing, and the scattering of a little spirit on the water, &c., &c. They have a belief in a future state, as on the death of any leading man or one of any position it is customary to bury with him a quantity of his property, which may consist of coral, cowries, silk, guns, &c., but a considerable portion of which is stolen by his immediate relatives before the grave is finally closed up.

I have argued and reasoned with the more intelligent of them on this subject, and pointed out that they know as well as myself such things can only decay and rot. and do not accompany their late owners to the next world. They reply, saying : "My friend, I sabby them thing you tell me be true," and they continue to explain in "pigeon" English that the virtue and spirit of the goods in question have passed with the spirit of the departed into the next world.

Black and White.   CONSULAR COURT HOUSE, BENIN.—ROYAL NIGER COAST PROTECTORATE.

When a free-born man dies at a distance from the neighbourhood of his own house, whenever practicable he is always taken back to be buried there.

A plurality of wives is the universal custom of the country and they usually appear to live in harmony, the number varying from two to five hundred, according to the position or wealth of the individual.

Miss Kingsley writes in her recently-published valuable work, *Travels in West Africa:* "Since 1893 I have been collecting information in its native state regarding 'fetish,' and I use the usual terms, 'fetish' and 'ju-ju,' because they have among us a certain fixed value—a conventional, but a useful one. Neither 'fetish' nor 'ju-ju' are native words. 'Fetish' comes from the word by which the old Portuguese explorers used to designate the objects they thought the natives worshipped, and in which they were wise enough to recognise a certain similarity to their own little images and relics of saints, Feitiço. 'Ju-ju,' on the other hand, is French, and comes from the word for a toy or doll, so it is not so applicable as the Portuguese name, for the native image is not a doll or toy, and has far more affinity to the image of a saint, inasmuch as it is not venerated for itself or treasured because of its prettiness, but only because it is the residence or the occasional haunt of a spirit."

I give you a portrait of Miss Kingsley. Having the honour of being a personal friend I took the liberty of asking her for her photo. to enable me to produce the same, as I said I should so much like to present the "Queen of West African Travellers" to you. She answered me with a most emphatic "No! you certainly shall not have a likeness of me if you intend to say such things as that. If you will enter into a bond to say: Ladies and Gentlemen,—Here you see the portrait of an ordinary commonsense individual, usually referred to in West Africa as 'Our Aunt,' who went to the West Coast full of prejudices against us, and who now repents and owns up that there are, and have been in the past, sterling good men doing great work in developing English interest and commerce in that

MISS KINGSLEY

Black and White.   (Author of _Travels in West Africa_).

rapidly-improving country." I can only say that Miss Kingsley has adapted herself to every startling circumstance arising in the course of her travels, and endeared herself to all who had the pleasure of travelling with her, and who are looking forward to the future in hopes of seeing her again on the coast.

On the death of a native of Warri or Benin the whole of his wives, slaves, and all property is divided between the sons, the wives the same as any other goods or chattels or personal estate. A case bearing on this division of slaves, &c., I might quote in point. Nyowrie, the late chief of Warri, placed in my care a very pretty slave boy about twelve years of age, whom I brought to this country. I lent him to Mrs. Bancroft to carry the train of her dress in the play, "The School for Scandal," and he became a great favourite and thoroughly Europeanised, living for some time at Mrs. Bancroft's house. On his returning with me to Benin some time later I found his late master had died, and the sons, counting over the property of the deceased, included my very esteemed black *valet de chambre*, and demanded his surrender at my hands. Being more than reluctant to relinquish possession of him they took him away by force ; and, after being the pet and admiration of very many ladies and friends, being at that time one of the most interesting little negroes ever seen, he ultimately degenerated into the unsophisticated slave, confined to a canoe paddling almost continually to and from the native markets of his own country.

I am not writing a book, but only giving a general sketch of " Benin and the surrounding country," and I cannot, in the course of a lecture, deal with all the many points I would under other circumstances. I should be occupying too much time if I described the climate, fauna and flora, the country the constant supply of slaves come from, how they are obtained in barter by the "down river" natives and description of goods paid for them, the food and drink consumed, the manner in which the more prominent men obtain so many wives, the diseases of the country, native medicines, &c., and trial by "sass" water (a pretty well-known poison).

PRESENTING A PETITION TO THE KING AND QUEEN OF SOBO.

DEATH OF CHIEF "LONG JOHN," OF BONNY.

There are no vultures, carrion crows, or birds of prey in the whole country, as in Bombay and other parts of the world. Consequently the remains of the slaves so numerously sacrificed at Benin are untouched by such, though I am not sure it might be better did they exist, horrible as the idea may be. They are numerous in Sierra Leone, where they prove good scavengers and are unmolested by the inhabitants.

Benin River is distant 4,380 miles from Liverpool, and is situated in 5° 50″ north latitude and 5° 10″ east longtitude, and Old Benin 6° 45″ north and 5° east.

I might be asked what is my opinion of the future of this great fertile part of West Africa of almost unlimited dimensions. It is always somewhat difficult to look into the future, and, though Artemus Ward's advice was, "Do not prophecy unless you know," nevertheless my firm impression is that at no distant date the whole of the rich territories of the Royal Niger Company and the Niger Coast Protectorate will be embodied with the adjacent British colony of Lagos under one Government, and, when it is developed as South Africa is being to day by railways, &c., it will prove in the future to be of almost equal wealth and importance ; and, though not a home for the labouring classes of Europe, still a great outlet for all heads of departments similar to India. Railways will carry civilisation, development, and progress wherever they go, and will find full employment for centuries to come, in not only bringing the rich products of the interior to the coast for shipment to Great Britain, but create such an outlay and demand for our manufactures which will give employment to all our surplus population.

In my early experience of the Niger and Niger Coast Protectorate regions, the only items of produce shipped home were palm oil, a little shea butter (a native grease), ebony, and ivory. Now we are getting large quantities not only of these but rubber, gum copal and various other gums, Beni seed, Chili peppers, palm kernels, coffee, cocoa, mahogany, gutta percha, mandioca flour, balsam, capsicums, castor oil seed, bark, patchouli, piassava, indigo, hides, shea nuts, ground nuts, kino raffia, kirandiffe, &c.

Black and White.

THE RIVER BENIN.

The world at large is too prone to think and speak of the African as the personification of idleness and laziness. It is a gross libel on the race; my experience is the reverse. I could give you many instances in proof of my views. Take the natives of the whole of the Kroo Coast, a large line of territory lying between Sierra Leone and the Gold Coast; they do the whole of the work at the various European factories and trading establishments on the West Coast. Our cruisers on the African station take a great number as an addition to their crews, and they do all the heaviest and hardest work, pulling boats, cleaning and coaling the ships, &c.; the same also applies to all the mail and merchant steamers traversing that coast.

Then again, some tens of thousands of tons of palm kernels are annually exported from the West Coast of Africa, and each small nut is taken separately, and the shell, which is of very great strength and hardness, is cracked by hand; no one can realise the labour necessary to break, separate, and prepare only a few pounds of these.

The moment rubber was discovered the natives rushed by thousands to gather every possible pound of it, and tedious work it is. See the native heavy cloth made at and near Kano, near the Niger, the raw cotton grown by themselves; also the weaving and dyeing by indigo. Nearly fifty years ago Dr. Barth estimated the produce of this at the enormous total of millions, and these country-made cloths in various sizes and qualities find their way in large quantities to Alexandria, Tripoli, Tunis, Morocco, and every port and place nearly in Western Africa, as well as at all intermediate central places *en route*. It is estimated that Kano-made gowns called "tobes," and other of their home-made cotton fabrics, clothe one-half the population of the Central Soudan.

See the constant traffic of the tens of thousands of natives across the desert to and from various points, and whose journeys occupy from three to nine months; realize, if you can, their patience, endurance, labour, and suffering. Dr. Barth travelled with a caravan consisting of 3,000 camels, laden exclusively with salt.

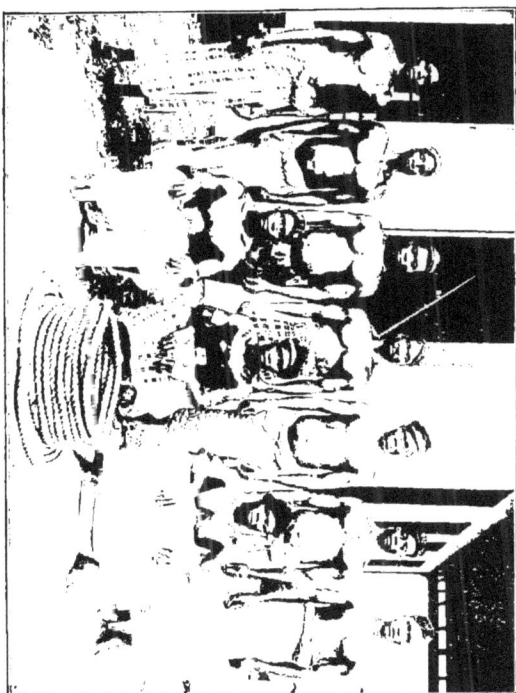

KROOMAN TUG-OF-WAR TEAM.

Black and White.

Need I go further and point to the industrious African
negroes working in the Southern States of America, now happily
all free labourers, and producing beautiful balls of snow-white
cotton in incalculable quantities, and so cheap that, with all its
numerous attendant expenses, it can be sold in this country at
3d. to 4d per pound

I should weary you by quoting much more in favour of my
argument against the unjust charge of idleness and laziness of
the negro. Cultivate and create wants in him, and you will find
he has all the ambition of the white race to live on a par with
and be equal with his neighbour.

The late Bishop Crowther, who worked so long and
earnestly in the cause of the Church Missionary Society, was
himself a slave, rescued from a slave ship ; so also was the
late respected Hon. Sybil Boyle, of Sierra Leone, and I could
quote numerous other similar instances proving the comparatively easy possibility of raising the native of Africa to a
high social level.

In conclusion, I would like to remind my hearers that
Britain owes an enormous debt to Africa. The truth is not
always palatable, nor is it at all times wise to put it forth ;
but the great debt I allude to took a great number of years
to incur, and was swollen in volume year by year for centuries.
I allude to the slave trade carried on under the English flag,
and considered a trade to be proud of—in fact, I have heard
of the church bells being rung in Liverpool to commemorate
the safe return of a ship to this port at the completion of
a prosperous slave-trading voyage; and some of you will
remember a celebrated actor on the stage of a Liverpool
theatre, when the audience showed some signs of disapproval
of him, reminding them that at that time there was hardly
a brick joined to another in their town that was not cemented
with the blood of a slave, meaning, of course, that most of the
money in Liverpool was made, directly or indirectly, out of their
traffic in slaves.

We have it on record that the English flag flew for num-
berless years—certainly one hundred and more—over the

A PARTY OF WOUNDED BLUEJACKETS AND MARINES ON BOARD SHIP,
AFTER A BRUSH WITH A TROUBLESOME CHIEF.

Graphic.

annual exportation of about 16,000 slaves from the Bonny
River alone, and the flags of other countries combined with our
own over the annual export of as many from Benin. During
the sixty years ending with 1847, 1,462,000 slaves were
transported from Africa to America alone.

I am not here to-night to give a lecture on the extent and
horrors of the slave trade carried on by England in the past,
but to remind you, as I would all English-speaking people, that
Africa has been brought more or less into this terrible state of
savagery and degradation by our own huge traffic across the
seas in human flesh, as we set almost every man's hand against
his neighbour's in Africa to procure slaves to fill our ships.
Each one shipped by us probably cost the lives of five to ten
others, counting the fire, rapine, slaughter, and deaths by the
long tedious march to the coast, &c., &c.

Let England, then, set about paying off this gigantic debt
I have been trying to prove to you she owes to Africa. It took
centuries on our part to incur, and of such magnitude is it that
we shall take a long time to pay it off. It will prove a very
remunerative business, as I have already shown you what has
been done in Lagos, rescued as it has been within half a century
from a state similar to that in which Benin is to-day. Let us
build railways and develope these rich countries. Fortunately,
we have that far-seeing and able statesman, the Right Hon.
J. Chamberlain, with us, whom future generations both white
and black will bless for his foresight and efforts made in this
direction in the nineteenth century for the advancement and
welfare of Africa. I cannot pay too great a tribute to the
vigorous and bold policy he is displaying in this splendid work.

Six thousand labourers are at present employed making the
Congo Railway, a great portion of which is already completed.
All these are natives of the West Coast, and are found to be
excellent workmen. One thousand more labourers are still
required, which Messrs. Elder, Dempster & Co. will find no
difficulty in at once providing. The same remarks apply also
to the railways of Sierra Leone and Lagos, which are being
made under the direction of the Right Honourable Joseph

WAR CANOE.

Black and White.

Chamberlain. Other railways on the Coast are most urgently needed, and an ample supply of native labour, I am quite certain, will be readily found.

A few days ago I had the honour of presiding at a crowded meeting of the Royal Geographical Society in Liverpool addressed by Captain A. St. H. Gibbons, F.R.G.S., on "A Journey of Exploration in Central Africa," from which he has recently returned. It is to such intrepid travellers—I might almost say heroes, as they go with their lives in their hand, encountering every possible danger—that England owes her greatness, as they open out new fields for enterprise and commerce and add additional territory to our great empire.

I may not live to see the day, but some of the younger men present in this assembly to-day assuredly will, when Benin will be a grand, well-conducted, civilised, Christian, and British colony, exporting all the present and many more valuable products of the land, and when the startling horrible revelations of to-day will only be a matter of history.

Much as we may regret the very terrible disaster that has occurred, and we pour out our deepest sympathy with the afflicted relatives of those who have been so ruthlessly murdered, much good will result from the great evil. Though this will be a poor consolation to them, many hundreds of human beings will be annually spared crucifixion and torture, and the country become settled, peaceful, and prosperous.

———

Since these lectures were delivered Benin City has been taken by our forces, and Bida and Ilorin have surrendered to the Royal Niger Company.

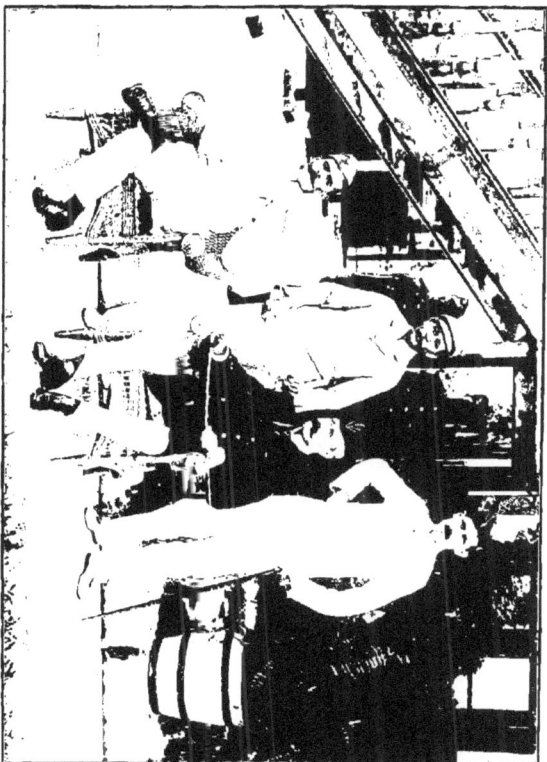

Black and White.

Mr. R. F. Locke
(one of the survivors).

The late Major Copland-Crawford
(massacred with the expedition to Benin)

GROUP OF NIGER COAST PROTECTORATE OFFICIALS.

IN FAR LAGOS.

THE officials of the Colony of Lagos in our illustration on the opposite page, taken from left to right and from top to foot, are:—Mr. J. G. Bly, Foreman of Works; Mr. F. C. Francis, Foreman of Works; Mr. G. W. Ambrose, District Commissioner; Mr. J. F. Thomas, Foreman of Works; Mr. J. F. Carroll, Assistant Commissioner of Police; Mr. J. A. Rowse, Assistant Surveyor; Major T. M. Hawtayne, Travelling Commissioner; Major A. McD. Moore, Special Service Officer; Mr. A. C. Stuart, Master of Government Vessels; Mr. F. H. Francis, Foreman of Works; Mr. G. H. Easton, Keeper of Prison; Mr. J. Nettleship, Book-keeper, Public Works Department; Lieutenant Cowie, The Haussa Force; Lieutenant L. N. Blackwell, The Haussa Force; Mr. W. M. Mackison, Sanitary Engineer; Mr. M. R. Menendez, District Commissioner; Mrs. Browne; Hon. C. H. H. Moseley, Colonial Treasurer; Miss O'Flynn, European Nurse; His Excellency Capt. G. C. Denton, C.M.G., Acting Governor; His Honour T. C. Rayner, Chief Justice; Mr. H. B. H. Chapman, Director of Public Works; Mr. F. P. Pinkett, Acting District Commissioner; Mr. E. Ehrhardt, Police Magistrate; Mr. S. K. Hayward, Engineer of Government Vessels; Dr. F. G. Hopkins, Assistant Colonial Surgeon; Captain G. C. Gordon, The Haussa Force; Dr. C. W. Rowland, Chief Medical Officer; Hon. G. Stallard, Queen Advocate; Mrs. Mark Kerr; Mrs. Denton; Hon. F. Rohrweger, Acting Colonial Secretary; Miss L. H. Clarke, European Nurse; Capt. R. E. D. Campbell, The Haussa Force; Mr. G. R. Powrie, Foreman of Works; Mr. C. W. Browne, Foreman of Works; Capt. J E. Cochrane, Private Secretary and A.D C.; Mr. F. W. Marshall, Local Auditor; Mr. Mark Kerr, Assistant Colonial Secretary; Mrs. Moseley; Dr. McDonnell, Assistant Colonial Surgeon; Mr. William McKenzie, Boilermaker; and Capt. Humphry, The Haussa Force.

OFFICIALS OF THE COLONY OF LAGOS.

Black and White.

From a photo. by Holm, Accra.

* 9 7 8 3 3 3 7 4 2 7 8 0 1 *